ALL ABOUT THE REPTILES OF THE WORLD

ANIMAL BOOKS

Children's Animal Books

BABY PROFESSOR
EDUCATION KIDS

Speedy Publishing LLC
40 E. Main St. #1156
Newark, DE 19711
www.speedypublishing.com

Animals that are cold-blooded are reptiles. Most of them lay eggs and their skin is comprised of dry, hard scales. Read further to learn more about the them and learn about some of the different species of reptiles.

Animals that are not able to maintain a constant body temperature automatically are known to be cold-blooded. They lay in the sun in order to heat up their bodies. In addition, this means that they do not burn energy to keep their body warm and they do not need nearly as much food as mammals or other similar sized warm-blooded animals.

Tokay gecko (Gekko gecko).

Close-up of the skin of a chameleon.

TYPES OF REPTILES

Reptiles come in many different types. The main species are crocodiles and alligators, turtles, lizards, and snakes. You can find them on each continent other than Antarctica.

Crocodiles and alligators may look big and slow, but they can move quite quickly when they attack.

Snakes are reptiles that are legless. They move around by flexing their body and even though they do not have legs, they can move quite quickly as well. There are only a small percentage of snakes that are poisonous. Many of them are known as constrictors, which means that they are able to squeeze their prey using their bodies until it is immobile or dead. They will then swallow it whole. If the prey is big, the snake can go weeks or possibly months without the need to eat again.

Colorful Blue Venomous Bush Viper Snake in Hollow Log.

Lizards are somewhat similar to snakes, but they have legs.

Turtles are considered reptiles as well, and they have a hard shell for protection. Some of them can live more than 100 years.

A Pogona lizard sitting on a wooden surface in a forest.

A man touches a large leatherback sea turtle.

THE SMALLEST, THE BIGGEST, AND THE FASTEST

The salt water crocodile is the biggest reptile and can grow up to 12 ½ feet long and 2,000 pounds.

The heaviest snake is the **GREEN ANACONDA,** and the longest snake is the **RETICULATED PYTHON.**

The **KOMODO DRAGON** is the biggest lizard.

The **LEATHERBACK TURTLE** is the largest turtle and can have an 8-foot-long shell and weight about 1,800 pounds.

The MINI CHAMELEON which is from Madagascar is the smallest reptile and will only grow to about an inch in length.

The THREAD SNAKE is the smallest snake and only grows to be about 4 inches long.

The SPINY TAILED IGUANA is thought to be the fastest reptile and can run up to about 20 miles an hour. The BLACK MAMBA is the fastest snake.

A juvenile Brookesia Micra standing on a human finger tip.

Black Mamba (Dendroaspis polylepis).

IS IT A REPTILE OR AMPHIBIAN?

The amphibians and reptiles are separated by a few differences. Amphibians will go through what is known as a larval stage, similar to a tadpole turning into a frog. This is not the case with reptiles. Reptiles will have scales for skin and amphibians have a moist, glandular skin.

Some examples of amphibians are toads, salamanders and frogs.

American Crocodiles.

LET'S TAKE A CLOSER LOOK AT DIFFERENT TYPES OF REPTILES

CROCODILES AND ALLIGATORS

As you learned earlier, both crocodiles and alligators are reptiles, are cold-blooded, and regulate the temperature of their body using the surrounding environment. Alligators will cool off by sitting in the water or the shade and warm up using the sun. Like most other reptiles, they lay eggs and their skin is comprised of hard, dry scales.

Alligators are often referred to as gators and crocodiles are referred to as crocs.

IS IT A CROCODILE OR AN ALLIGATOR?

The best way to tell the difference is to look at the width of their snout. The alligator has a broad, wide nose and the crocodile will typically have a narrow one. Generally, alligators are darker in color.

Chinese Alligator.

You will find alligators near fresh water environments. There are only the two types of alligators (the Chinese Alligator and the American Alligator) and there are only two countries around the world where they can be found; the United States and China. In the United States, alligators can be found in the southeast, mostly in Louisiana and Florida.

Basking American Alligator.

Crocodiles can be found in tropical areas such as Australia, Asia, Africa and America. There are some crocodiles that are able to live in both saltwater and freshwater.

Little baby crocodiles hatching from eggs.

KOMODO DRAGON

He is a fearsome and giant lizard and its scientific name is Varanus komodoensis.

They are the largest lizard species throughout the world and are able to grow to be 10 feet long and up to 300 pounds.

Komodo Dragon Reptile.

Its skin is scaly and is speckled brownish yellow in color which allows it to be difficult to see when it is still. The Komodo Dragon has stubby, short legs with a giant tail which is the same length as its body. It has a long yellow forked tongue and 60 serrated sharp teeth.

Komodo Dragon looking up.

SEA TURTLES

Sea turtles are the turtles that reside within the ocean. The different types can be found in every ocean throughout the world except the Arctic Ocean, as it is too cold for them to live. Typically, they prefer the warmer seas and will stay in the shallow coastal areas like bays and lagoons, however occasionally they can be found in the deeper parts of the ocean as well.

Green Sea Turtle (Chelonia mydas).

Sea turtles are categorized in the same class of animals as a reptile. This means that they breathe air, are cold-blooded, they lay eggs, and have scaly skin. There are seven different types of sea turtles. The types are loggerhead, olive ridley, leatherback, hawksbill, green, flatback, and Kemp's ridley sea turtles. The Black Sea turtle is sometimes considered to be an eighth species of the sea turtle.

Hawksbill Sea Turtle.

EASTERN DIAMONDBACK RATTLER

This rattlesnake is one the largest venomous snakes throughout the world and at eight feet long, is certainly the largest of the Americas. They are related to the snake family known as pit vipers. They have tiny temperature-sensing pits on each side of their head that helps them to find prey in the dark.

Eastern Diamondback Rattlesnake.

The Eastern Diamondback Rattler lives in the southeastern section of the United States and live in all different types of habitats from marshes to forests. They like to live within burrows that have been created by mammals, like gophers.

Tail of Eastern Diamondback Rattlesnake (Crotalus adamanteus).

The Eastern Diamondback Rattler is a very dangerous, venomous, and aggressive snake. They are able to strike quickly and can reach out for about two thirds of the length of their body. An adult rattler is able to control the amount of venom that it releases so the effectiveness of the strike varies. A baby rattler has a bite that is even more potent and might continue to strike releasing a greater amount of venom because of its lack of control. In either instance, a person bit by this snake should immediately seek medical attention.

Eastern Diamondback Rattlesnake

GREEN ANACONDA SNAKE

This snake is the largest one throughout the world. Typically, when a person uses the term Anaconda, they are referring to this species of snake.

It can be found in South America closer to the equator in the northern part of the country. They live in several countries including Columbia, Brazil, Venezuela, Bolivia and Ecuador.

Green Anaconda (Eunectes murinus).

They enjoy living in areas of water since they are good swimmers, however it is difficult for them to move around on land. Their habitats include swamps, marshes, and other areas that have slow-moving waters in a tropical rain forest.

Green Anaconda (Eunectes murinus).

GREEN IGUANA

The Green Iguana is a lizard that is fairly large and is popular as a domestic pet.

It is native to South America into some areas of central and North America and typically it lives in the rain forests up in the trees. It can also be found in the United States in the wild due to pets being released back into the wild or escaping back into the wild.

Green Iguana.

They are known to grow up to 20 pounds and 6 feet long in captivity, which is a pretty good size for a lizard. Their tail is about half the length of their body.

Even though they are referred to as ***"green"*** iguanas, they can be found in other colors and shades besides green that include orange, purple and blue. Their skin color acts as a camouflage, which allows them to blend into the landscape. Their skin is waterproof and tough.

Green Iguana.

KING COBRA SNAKE

This snake is the longest venomous one throughout the world. It is known for its fierceness and can be extremely dangerous.

The King cobra can be found in southeast Asia including areas of India and other countries such as Thailand, Burma, Indonesia and the Philippines. They enjoy living in the forest and being near water. They are able to swim well and can quickly move on land and in trees.

King Cobra

They normally grow to about 13 feet long, however there have been sightings on King Cobras up to 18 feet. Its color is tan, dark green, or black having yellow bands down the length of its body. Its belly is a cream color with black bands.

King Cobra.

The King Cobra's venom isn't the most lethal, however they are still known to be one of the deadlier snakes due to the amount of venom they are able to distribute in a single bite. The amount of venom from a single bite can kill 20 grown men or even an elephant.

For additional information about the different species of reptiles, you can go to your local library, research the internet, and ask questions of your teachers, family and friends.

www.ingramcontent.com/pod-product-compliance
Ingram Content Group UK Ltd.
Pitfield, Milton Keynes, MK11 3LW, UK
UKHW062356281025
8631UKWH00046B/424

9 798869 437983